30 Minutes
... To Prepare
the Perfect CV

Lynn Williams

KOGAN
PAGE

First published in 2002

Kogan Page Limited
120 Pentonville Road
London N1 9JN
UK

British Library Cataloguing in Publication Data
A CIP record for this book is available from the British Library.
ISBN 0 7494 3785 5

Typeset by Saxon Graphics Ltd, Derby
Printed and bound in Great Britain by Clays Ltd, St Ives plc

CONTENTS

INTRODUCTION

Your CV

Imagine your CV was just one of a stack of 600–700. Imagine just 10 would be chosen for interview. How successful would yours be? Is it easy to read, easy to understand and memorable? Does it state your relevant skills, qualifications and achievements clearly and succinctly? Would it inspire a prospective employer to want to meet you?

The aim of your CV

The aim of a CV is, purely and simply, to get you an interview. To achieve this, your CV needs to:

● display your relevant skills and qualities clearly;
● attract interest;
● make a good impression.

1

PLANNING YOUR CV

The purpose of your CV is to motivate a prospective employer to want to interview you by demonstrating clearly that you have the right skills and experience for the job you want. A good CV will show that you:

- understand the particular requirements of the job;
- have the specific skills needed;
- have the right sort of experience;
- have the necessary personal qualities.

The three key points to keep in mind when planning your CV are:

- **Keep it short**. No more than two A4-sized pages made up of short, succinct sections illustrating your skills and experience.
- **Keep it clear**. Make it easy to read with clear section headings and a well-organized layout that presents the information in a logical, easy to follow style.

- **Keep it relevant**. An employer has only one question in mind when looking for a potential employee:

  Can this person do the job?

Look at it from the employer's point of view

The average employer looking through a stack of CVs usually has less than 20 seconds to scan the page and decide whether it goes in the 'yes' or 'no' pile. They consequently have to narrow their interest to specific points:

- Does this applicant have the skills required for the job?
- Do they have experience relevant to the job?
- Have they got the right personal qualities for the job?
- Do they understand the specific needs of the job?

Make your CV relevant

Make your CV easy to choose for the 'yes' pile by ensuring it answers those questions. When you're planning your CV, be clear about the skills, experience and personal qualities you have, and make sure they come across strongly:

- **Highlight your skills and experience**. Your relevant skills, qualifications and experience are the most important things in your CV. Match them as closely as possible to those required by the job and put them on the front page.
- **State your achievements**. Make your achievements clear – a CV is not the place for false modesty. Employers don't have time to hunt for information; they need to be able to see at a glance exactly what you have to offer.

- **Keep it simple and direct**. Cut out unnecessary details that will only obscure stronger points. Stick to clear statements in plain language.

What you can leave out

- **Avoid unnecessary personal details**. The more irrelevant information you can eliminate, the more clearly your skills, qualifications and experience will stand out. The following items can safely be omitted:
  - marital status;
  - maiden name;
  - number of children;
  - ages of children;
  - nationality;
  - gender;
  - partner's occupation;
  - religious affiliation;
  - political affiliation;
  - age;
  - previous salary;
  - reasons for leaving jobs;
  - names and addresses for references.

- **Avoid negative information**. Always put things in the most positive way you can. It's unwise (and unprofitable) to lie or bend the truth on your CV, but be careful about including things that will diminish your chance of getting an interview. If they don't affect your ability to do the job, leave them out until you can explain the circumstances face-to-face with your prospective employer.

- **Avoid out-of-date information**. Your potential employer is interested in what you are doing now and what you intend to do in the future. Things that happened more than a decade or so ago are unlikely to be relevant unless they directly affect your current capabilities. Keep the front page of your CV for more noteworthy information.

Create the right effect

Make a businesslike impression. Your CV should be printed clearly using:

- black ink;
- good quality paper:
  - 100 gsm weight;
  - white or cream in colour;
  - A4 sized.

Check spelling and grammar thoroughly before you print it out. The layout of your CV, the way it's arranged on the page, is important too. A good layout will make the finished document much easier to read.

Include:

- wide margins;
- clear and logical spacing;
- discrete capital letters, underlining, bold print and italics to emphasize key points.

Avoid:

- obscure, hard to read typefaces or fonts;
- fancy borders or other decoration;
- alterations and amendments on the page (if anything needs to be changed, correct the original and print off a new copy);

- photographs, personal citations, or anything gimmicky and unprofessional.

Finally, when sending out your CV:

- send it well before the closing date;
- send it to a named person. If you don't have a name, ring the company switchboard and ask;
- include a covering letter written specifically for that job, summarizing and re-emphasizing your key points;
- like your CV, the letter must be printed in a clear, unfussy typeface on good quality plain white or cream A4 paper;
- you can also use the covering letter for points specifically asked for in the job advertisement that you wouldn't normally put in your CV – current salary, for example;
- send letter and CV unfolded in a white A4-size envelope.

Example CVs – before and after

Compare the 'before' version of this CV with the 'after' one to see how basic information can be strengthened and highlighted to give a CV that:

- states relevant skills and qualities clearly;
- attracts interest;
- makes a good impression.

Example 1 – before

CURRICULUM VITAE

SURNAME: PERRIS
FORENAMES: JOY HELEN MARY (FEMALE)
AGE: 32
DATE OF BIRTH: 12/5/72
NATIONALITY: BRITISH
DEPENDENTS: 3 CHILDREN; AGES: 12; 8; 5
MARITAL STATUS: SEPARATED PENDING DIVORCE
ADDRESS: 27 KINGSCOTE PLACE, LIMPNEY, SURREY,
SR1 2AA
TELEPHONE: 00000 000000

EDUCATION
September 1977–July 1983
Porton Infants and Junior School

September 1983–July 1988
Porton Comprehensive: obtained GCSE passes in English Language,
English Literature, Needlework, Biology, History, Maths

October 1993–June 1995
South London College: German GCSE (Evening Class); Pass

September 2000–Present
Limpney Training Centre: CLAIT and Clerical Skills Course

EMPLOYMENT HISTORY
1997–1999 – Mutual Assurance Association
General Office Administrator

1992–1997 – Clipper Retail
Shop Assistant, rising to Duty Manager

1988–1992 – Danube Imports Ltd
Clerical Assistant

HOBBIES AND INTERESTS
I enjoy music, dancing and aerobics, and was a keen member of the
parent governors' committee.

Example 2 – after

JOY PERRIS
27 Kingscote Place
Limpney, Surrey, SR1 2AA
Tel: 00000 000000

Career profile
An experienced administrator, supervisor and office manager with a high
degree of initiative and self-motivation, who enjoys the challenge of a
busy, demanding work environment, with the ability to maintain a
consistently high standard of work under pressure.

Key skills
- Supervising staff
- Implementing standard procedures accurately
- Prioritizing workload
- Proficient German
- Computer skills – Microsoft Office:
    - Word
    - Excel
    - PowerPoint
    - Outlook

Career history
2000–Present   Limpney Training Centre
CLAIT and NVQ level 3 – Clerical Skills Course; Administration and
Supervision.
Advanced course to update and extend computer and office management
skills, including Information Technology.

1997–1999   Mutual Assurance Association
Office Administrator – Responsible for collation and administration of
documents and records; the organization of data within the department;
dealt with queries to the department.

1992–1997   Clipper Retail
Duty Manager – Supervised staff and attended to customers in busy city-centre store. Responsible for daily administration of section including stock control, section turnover, and customer complaints. Promoted from Retail Assistant.

1988–1992   Danube Imports Ltd
Clerical Assistant – Dealt with office administration including bookkeeping and invoicing.

Education and training
Porton Comprehensive – Six GCSE passes including English and Maths
South London College – GCSE pass in German
Limpney Training Centre – CLAIT and NVQ3 Clerical Skills

Personal details
Date of birth – 12 May 1972
Health – Non-smoker
Licence – Full, clean UK licence
Interests – Music, dancing, aerobics. Served as a Parent Governor on primary school Governing Body; involved in decisions on budgets, curriculum, and other management issues.

Although it's a little longer, the revised CV still only runs to two pages and manages to put the most relevant information about job skills and career history on the first page, leaving the less important facts about education and personal details for the second page. Note that the revised CV:

- gives much more information;

- gives more relevant information – things an employer will want to know;

- clearly highlights skills and experience;

- puts key, relevant skills in an at-a-glance section that's hard to miss;

- is much easier to read;

- looks substantially more professional.

2

COMPILING YOUR CV

Your CV needs to:

- be easy to read;
- be easy to understand;
- be attractive;
- present your skills, strengths and achievements clearly;
- encourage the reader to want to interview you.

Think of your CV as a newspaper – you need an attention-grabbing front page that gives the headline news and major points, with the follow-up story on page two. Remember that an employer may only spend 20 seconds reading your CV on the initial scan-through. Tell them what they *most* need to know on the front page and assume that they are not, at this stage, even going to get to the second!

Page one

Name, address and telephone number

Your name needs to stand out clearly at the head of your CV. Include your home address, telephone number including area code, and private e-mail address. Be wary of putting your work e-mail address unless your current employer knows you are looking for another job and is happy for you to receive private e-mail at work.

Personal statement

Include this on your CV where it will help show your relevant skills and aptitudes more prominently. There are three main types:

- **Personal profile**. A short statement of around 30 words outlining your key personal characteristics.

- **Career profile**. A concise outline of your career highlights and work experience.

- **Career objective**. A statement about the specific career or employment position you are aiming for. This can be particularly useful if you are starting your career, returning to work after a break, or changing career direction.

Key points

Highlight your most important skills, achievements or qualifications by putting them in a separate, easy-to-read, hard-to-ignore section. Depending on what is most relevant to your position, you could entitle the section:

- **Key skills** – outlining your main skills relevant to the job you are applying for;

- **Key qualifications** – stating your academic, technical or professional training relevant to the position;

- **Key achievements** – showing your chief career accomplishments and suggesting your ability to achieve similar results in the post you are applying for.

Your current job

This really has to go on the front page; the rest of your career history can follow overleaf. Include:

- dates of employment;
- name of employer;
- job title;
- a short description of your responsibilities;
- your key achievements in that position (if you haven't already put them in the previous section). Point out the advantages of employing you and include achievements such as:

  - increased productivity;
  - increased sales or profits;
  - improved customer relations;
  - reduced staff turnover;
  - improved design;
  - increased efficiency;
  - winning an award;
  - improved public profile;
  - improved employee relations.

Page two

Career history

Continue the details of your employment history. The further back in your career you go, the less relevant the information becomes and the less detail you need to go into.

Education and training

Include:

- work-related training gained in your job;
- academic qualifications – GCSE, HND, HNC, BSc, BA, PhD, MSc, etc;
- professional qualifications;
- vocational training, if relevant;
- technical training.

It's also worth including any training or skills with a general value that could be useful in most jobs, such as:

- language skills – define as conversational, business, bilingual or fluent;
- computer skills – name packages used, Word, Outlook, etc;
- first-aid training;
- driving licence.

Personal details

This section includes:

- your date of birth – you don't need to put your age as well;
- interests and hobbies – give brief details especially if they add to or support your stated skills and qualities;
- special details – you might want to include, for example:
  - nationality if a foreign national or dual nationality;
  - registered disability;
  - marital status or gender if strict (and legal) requirement of the job;
  - if you're prepared to relocate;
  - if you're a non-smoker;
  - possession of a full, clean, UK driver's licence.

Divide the information on your CV into short, clearly headed sections, so it's easy to read, easy to understand and easy to absorb the main facts.

Example 1

PAULINE KING
51 St Andrews Road
Oldlands, Northampton NT14 8FV
Tel: 00000 000000
e-mail: pnking@anyisp.co.uk

Career profile
(Pauline has chosen a career profile to focus attention on her career highlights and experience.)

A widely experienced sales professional with a specific understanding of business-to-business negotiations and a proven track record in business systems, office supplies and business machines.

Key achievements
(Pauline has chosen to include a section on her key achievements to follow up the statements in her career profile with specific facts and figures.)

- Increased market share of Rexolite business machines from 12 per cent to 17 per cent within nine months

- Maintained or increased market share year on year

- Recruited and trained sales team that won Rexolite top company award

- Raised profile and increased enquiries at Harben Copier Products by 15 per cent

- Achieved 20 per cent increase in technical support uptake

- Took direct sales operation from start-up to profitability within 18 months

- Increased sales by up to 12 per cent annually

- Consistently met and exceeded targets

17

Career summary

1998 to Present

Rexolite Business Machines

Sales Manager

Responsible for own territory plus sales team of six. Successfully planned marketing campaign for sales promotion. Set team budget, assigned territories and targets, monitored sales statistics, undertook staff review and training.

(Because Pauline has included a separate Key achievements section, she doesn't need to repeat her accomplishments here.)

----

end of first page

1994 to 1998

Harben Copier Products Ltd

Sales Executive

Successfully targeted technical support services for business machines with resulting increase in turnover. Coordinated annual trade show attracting orders exceeding £200K. Increased sales of original models plus handled successful introduction of two new digital models.

1990 to 1994

Office Direct Ltd

Sales Representative

Responsible for start-up of direct sales operation. Developed virgin territory. Planned marketing campaigns and sales promotions. Planned and undertook telephone sales operation. Took area into profitability within 18 months.

1984 to 1990

Various

Sales Representative

Telesales

Retail Sales

Responsible for all aspects of sales in a variety of environments both face-to-face and over the phone, dealing with both public and business enquiries.

(Pauline has summarized her early experience rather than go into detail. None of the experience or achievements she attained in these positions outweighs that of subsequent jobs so she's left them out so they don't obscure her recent, relevant accomplishments. This will also help to keep her CV down to two pages.)

Education and training

Member of the Professional Sales Society
Member of the Women's Marketing Network
(Pauline has included two professional associations she belongs to.)

Institute of Business, Sales and Marketing
1997 – Diploma in Sales Management
1989 – Diploma in Marketing

Cornwell CFE
1984 – Certificate of Business Studies

St Michael High School
1982 – Seven GCSEs including Maths, French and English
(Pauline has cut out details of her GCSEs as being too long ago and irrelevant. Subsequent qualifications usually make GCSEs immaterial. Most employers are, in any case, only interested in Maths and English – which show that you are numerate and articulate – and any languages or specific qualifications relevant to the job – IT or Design Technology, for example.)

Personal details

Date of birth: 4 June 1966
Licence: Full, clean, UK driver's licence
(A clean driving licence is important to people in sales where there's often a lot of travelling involved.)
Health: Excellent; non-smoker
(Not an essential statement, but many companies prefer non-smokers these days because of health issues.)
Interests : Fine art and antiques

Example 2

SYLVIA PATTERSON
Flat 2 Moorlands House, Renwick Road
Headbury, Lincs LC21 7YH
Tel: 00000 000000
e-mail: pattersons@anyisp.co.uk

Personal profile
(Sylvia has used a personal profile to highlight her personal qualities.)

A punctual, reliable and efficient administrator with excellent secretarial and organizational skills, and experience of handling a variety of tasks proficiently, working both on own initiative and as part of a team.

Key skills
(Sylvia's practical skills are important, without them she couldn't do her job, so she highlights them in a Key skills section.)

- Keyboard skills – 60 wpm
- Computer skills Microsoft Office:
  – Word
  – PowerPoint
  – Outlook
  – Excel
- Excellent telephone manner
- Organizing and carrying out administrative work:
  – Preparing and writing routine correspondence
  – Maintaining records
  – Dealing with incoming mail and calls

Career history

2000–Ongoing	Headbury Resource Association

Secretary
Organized and administered voluntary association concerned with the allocation and use of amenities funding within the village:
(Because Sylvia is currently caring for small children, she doesn't have a full-time job. However, her voluntary work with the Tenants

*Association has given her valuable experience and extra skills useful in
any future employment. She therefore lists her responsibilities and
achievements in full.)*

- Represented the association at Parish Council and Local
  Government meetings, as well as meetings of other
  organizations and special interest groups
- Liaised with Parish Council and Local Council Office
- Drafted reports on specific issues as a member of various
  working parties
- Organized monthly meetings and Annual General Meetings
- Took minutes of meetings and wrote-up, printed and circulated
  to members
- Dealt with correspondence

----
end of first page

1999–Present
During this period I have been caring for my children full-time.

1994–1999   Tetbury Imports
Secretary
Responsible for secretarial support to department:

- Typed reports and correspondence
- Minuted all departmental meetings
- Organized appointments
- Arranged meetings
- Dealt with telephone enquiries and requests

1991–1994   Henbury White Ltd
Secretary
Clerical Assistant
Organized and carried out routine office administration,
maintained records and files, dealt with incoming mail, prepared
routine correspondence.
*(Because her duties with this employer add little to her skills or experi-
ence profile, Sylvia condenses her two positions with the company
together, and covers them very briefly.)*

Education and training

North Lincolnshire Open Learning Centre 1992

- Introduction to Computer Literacy
- Pitman Intermediate Office Practice

Moorlands College 1990–1991

- RSA Stage 1 Keyboard Skills
- RSA Stage 1 Office Skills
- Pitman Elementary Office Practice

Moorcross School 1985–1990
Seven GCSEs including Maths, English and Commerce

Personal details

Date of birth – 6 February 1974
Interests – Badminton, swimming
Licence – Full, clean UK driver's licence
References available on request

Example 3

JOHN FELLING
10 Abbots Drive
Abbots Stoke
Dean, Norfolk NF10 3ME
Tel: 00000 000000
e-mail johnfelling@anyisp.co.uk

Career objective

(John is looking for his first 'proper' job and puts a career objective at the top of his CV so it's clear to anyone reading it.)

A Biological Sciences graduate with a keen interest in the commercial application of basic research seeking a career in biotechnology, especially the pharmaceutical industry.

Key qualifications
(At this stage of his career, John's qualifications are a more important asset than his work experience.)

- BSc (Hons) Biological Sciences
- Year 3 modules include:
  - Molecular genetics
  - Prokaryotic biochemical systems
  - Use of recombinant DNA
  - Use of restriction enzymes
  - Population genetics
  - Industrial fermentation processes

(John highlights the relevant modules from his third year studies to show he has some understanding and practical experience in the field he wants to enter.)

Employment experience
(Any work experience is valuable if you are a school or college leaver. However good your academic qualifications, it's still useful for an employer to know you have successfully held down a job in the past. John will leave these out of his CV, however, when applying for subsequent jobs because they will no longer be relevant.)

Summer 2001
Portland Gallagher
Administrative Assistant

Summer 2000
Morton Electronics
Clerical Assistant

----
end of first page

Summer 1999
Morton Electronics
Clerical Assistant

Education and training
1999–2001 University of Birmingham
BSc (Hons) Biological Sciences

1992–1999 North Dean School
A levels – Maths, Biology, Chemistry
GCSEs – Seven including Maths and English

Computer skills

- PC Operating Systems – DOS and Windows
- Unix programming system
- Word
- Excel
- Access
- Novel NetWare

(Note that John includes the computer skills he has picked up at university under a separate heading. Computer skills often come in useful in a variety of jobs and are worth mentioning when you have them.)

Personal details

Date of birth – 18 May 1980
Interests – Reading, swimming and music, member of the University Athletics Club

3

TARGETING YOUR CV

If you want to make your CV really relevant, look at the job ad. When you find an ad for a vacancy you particularly desire, take a close look at the details and revise your CV using the ad for guidance. Look at:

- what they want;
- what you've got;
- how you can match your CV to their needs.

Advertisement

Personal assistant

A small private publisher urgently requires a mature, hard-working assistant to provide administrative and secretarial support. Must have excellent communication and organizational abilities. Keyboard skills (Microsoft Office Suite currently used) and a confident telephone manner essential. Experienced bookkeeper familiar with spreadsheets would be an advantage but training will be given to the right applicant. Understanding of environmental issues desirable. Must be able to work on own initiative without supervision and have a flexible approach to working hours.

They want:

- computer skills – preferably Microsoft Office;
- administrative and secretarial experience;
- excellent communication skills;
- confident telephone manner;
- some bookkeeping experience;
- familiarity with spreadsheets;
- understanding of environmental issues;
- ability to work on own initiative without supervision;
- flexible approach to working hours.

You can deduce from the ad they would also like someone:

- dependable and supportive;
- willing to learn and take on extra training;
- willing to be flexible and work outside a strict job description;
- confident and helpful;
- used to routine office work but able to cope with responsibility.

Use the ad to revise your CV

From your own skills, qualities and experience:

- select the skills, qualities and experience specifically requested;
- make sure these are clearly highlighted;
- use words and phrases that appear in the ad.

13350350750

Example CV – targeted approach

NAME

Address
Phone number

Personal profile
(Use key words from the advertisement.)
Experienced secretary, administrator, responsible, supportive,
flexible, confident

Key skills
(Include all you have that are mentioned in the ad.)

- Six years' experience in secretarial and administrative positions
- Computer skills – Microsoft Office:
  - Word for Windows
  - Excel spreadsheet package
  - Outlook Express
- Confident telephone manner
- Experience of working on own initiative
- Able to prioritize and organize own workload

Career history
(Link your responsibilities to those requested in the ad.)
Dates
Employer
Secretary
Provided secretarial and administrative support to department:

- Word-processed letters, reports and general correspondence
- Dealt with incoming mail
- Organized and coordinated appointments and bookings
- Maintained departmental diary
- Liaised with personnel in other offices
- Dealt with all general office administration

Dates
Employer
Secretary
(Brief outline of responsibilities or more details if relevant.)

Dates
Employer
Clerical Assistant
(Brief outline of responsibilities or more details if relevant.)

Education and training
(Brief outline or more details if relevant.)

Personal details
(Brief outline or more details if relevant. For example...)
Interests: Member of the Woodland Conservation Volunteer Trust
(Included because it shows some familiarity with environmental issues.)

4

JOB-RELATED CVS

Different jobs have different requirements when it comes to what makes a person right for that position. Some jobs require specific academic or technical qualifications, some call for certain personal qualities, while others demand a track record of achievement in that field.

This section shows how, by highlighting and calling attention to the relevant parts of your CV, you can effectively emphasize these key requirements. Remember, however, to keep the job advertisement or job description clearly in mind when deciding which are your most relevant skills for a specific job.

Each example uses the front page for key facts and high priority information, with back-up and lower-priority details on the second page.

The clerical CV

Office staff and administrators make sure a company operates professionally and effectively. When you apply for a clerical, secretarial or administrative job, make sure your CV highlights your:

- specific, practical clerical, administrative and organizational skills;
- experience;
- proficiency;
- ability to follow procedures and work effectively with others;
- dependability.

Example CV – for a clerical job

NANCY BURRELL
11 Lloyds Avenue, Park Green
Leeds LD12 7XO
Tel: 00000 000000

Personal profile

An experienced, highly trained **Personal Secretary** with first-rate shorthand and IT skills, excellent organizational skills and an understanding of the secretary's role in the current business world.

Key skills

- Secretarial skills:
  - Diploma in Secretarial and Administrative Studies
  - Keyboard – 75 wpm text and word-processing
  - Shorthand – 115 wpm
  - Audio transcription
  - Commercial correspondence
- Microsoft Office:
  - Word
  - Excel
  - PowerPoint
  - Outlook
- Other skills:
  - Internet and electronic mail systems
  - Financial software

Experience

An established track record in effective office support:

- Twelve years' secretarial experience
- Five years' experience as confidential secretary to CEO
- Committed to good office practice and procedures

Career summary

D C Bennett and Partners
1997–Present
Confidential Secretary
Provided full secretarial support:

- Typed letters, memoranda and reports with due regard for confidentiality
- Compiled monthly reports and statistics
- Organized meetings, took and typed minutes
- Arranged accommodation and travel for staff and overseas visitors
- Coordinated diary and appointments for MD
- Communicated with overseas clients

Solaris Holdings Ltd
1993–1997
Personal Secretary
Provided secretarial support to head of section

Purbright and Holland
1990–1993
Personal Secretary
Shorthand Typist

Education and training

1988–1990 Danes Cross College of Education
Diploma in Secretarial and Administrative Studies

1983–1988 Frenchay School
Five GCSEs including Maths, French and English

Personal details

Date of birth – 31 July 1972
Health – Non-smoker
Interests – Theatre and cinema; Member of St Giles dramatic society

The sales and marketing CV

Sales people make sure a company sells its products and services, and makes a profit. If you're applying for a sales or marketing job, highlight your:

- ability to sell;
- successful track record;
- drive and enthusiasm;
- confidence in your skills;
- integrity.

Example CV – for a sales job

ROGER HARUP
68 Orion Close, Aspen Hill
Staffordshire ST4 8SM
Tel: 00000 000000

Career profile

A sales professional with extensive experience in sales, marketing and management, the skill and confidence to identify and generate sales leads from a diverse prospect base, and a positive attitude towards the future.

Key experience

- Diploma in Marketing and E-commerce
- Three years' experience running a small international sales office
- Familiarity with export and UK commercial documentation
- Increased territory sales by 25 per cent in current position
- Increased net sales by 43 per cent

Career achievements

Staple & Dennis Ltd
1995 to Present
Commercial Manager
Responsible for Northern European sales operations:

- Recruited, motivated and developed staff
- Developed training and incentives
- Selected and trained representatives for overseas territories

- Managed existing accounts while developing new ones
- Maintained long-term customer relationships
- Increased repeat orders by 37 per cent
- Planned and controlled sales resources to maximum effect

Dakk Taylor & Co Ltd
1992 to 1995
Sales/Product Manager
- Increased sales year-on-year by up to 33 per cent
- Maintained cash flow and profitability
- Analysed and evaluated sales results
- Maintained profitability of product range and introduced and marketed new product ranges

PortMarine Ltd
1988 to1992
Sales Manager
Sales Representative
- Increased sales turnover
- Introduced new product and marketing ideas
- Recruited and trained sales team
- Promoted to Sales Manager in 1990

Education and training
Institute of Continuing Studies
Diploma in Marketing and E-Commerce
Diploma in Computing and IT

1981 to 1988 Stoke Croft School
A-levels: Maths and Economics
GCSEs: Six including Maths and English

Personal details
Date of birth	16 February 1970
Interests	IT and computing
Licence	Full, clean UK driving licence

References available on request

For another example of a sales CV, see Pauline King's on page 17.

The technical CV

Technical staff need to be able to carry out complex or tricky procedures proficiently, accurately and knowledge-ably. If your job is based on your technical proficiency, highlight your:

- qualifications and training;
- specific technical skills;
- experience, competence and expertise;
- dependability and accuracy;
- methodical, organized approach;
- ability to work with others as part of a team.

Example CV – for a technical job

Arta Peorra
Flat 2, Burston Court
Yealverstone, Kent KT14 2KP
Tel: 00000 000000
e-mail: apeorra@anyisp.co.uk

Career profile
A patient, perceptive and thorough research assistant, with a specific interest in molecular biology, especially cell signalling systems, and practical experience of eliciting, collecting and analysing biological data.

Key qualifications
- MSc Molecular Biology
- BSc Biochemistry

Key skills
- Knowledge of PCR, SSCP, SDS, PAGE and blotting techniques
- Background in cellular and molecular haematology
- Understanding of human molecular biology
- Experience in haematological cell signalling
- Coordinating, planning and running experiments
- Analysing data

Career history
Centre for Research into Biomedicine
1999–Present
Laboratory Assistant
Conducted research into mitogen activated protein kinase
phosphorylation in acute myoblastic leukaemic cells:

- Designed and organized experiments with aim of acquiring specific
  research data
- Undertook experimental procedures
- Collected and collated results
- Analysed preliminary data by computer
- Prepared preliminary report on findings

University of Sussex
1995–1999
Research Assistant
Research assistant to Professor Howard Fredrikson in the Department of
Oncology, investigating the molecular characteristics predictive of clini-
cal outcomes in patients with myeloblastic leukaemia.

Education and training
University of Sussex
MSc Molecular Biology
BSc Biochemistry (2.1)

Staple Hill School
A levels: Biology, Chemistry and Maths
GCSEs: Nine including Maths and English

Personal details
Date of Birth: 10 June 1974

Interests: Collecting clockwork models and automata; sailing

References available on request

The management CV

Managers make sure everything happens according to plan, and that staff carry out their work effectively and efficiently. If you're applying for a managerial job, emphasize your:

- personal qualities that make you a good manager;
- skill at managing and motivating others;
- ability to get results;
- problem-solving skills;
- interpersonal skills;
- experience, capability and dependability;
- drive and determination, and your enthusiasm, energy and commitment.

Example CV – for a management job

LIZ YATE
62 St Anthony's Lane
Staunton, Hertfordshire, HT3 7BE
Tel: 00000 000000

Personal profile

A proactive, result-orientated retail manager with significant experience in both sports and fashion environments. Excellent interpersonal skills, and the proven ability to manage and motivate staff.

Key skills and achievements

- Six years' experience in a fast-moving, multi-site retail environment
- Motivating and coaching staff to achieve and exceed sales targets
- Successfully introducing comprehensive staff training programmes
- Successfully introducing and implementing NK-kids and other promotional and public relations exercises

Career history

NKSport
1995 to Present
Retail Manager
Assistant Manager
Managing all facets of city-centre business, incorporating aspects of sport, leisure and fashion:

- Supervised operations
- Managed 10 permanent sales staff plus temporary staff
- Dealt with customer relations
- Handled accounts payable functions, inventory control and merchandise flow for total stock turnover of £1.2 million
- Developed staff training programmes to advance product knowledge and expertise, as well as current sales techniques
- Promoted to Retail Manager in 1998

David Davies, Leeds
1991 to 1995
Sales Supervisor
Sales Assistant

Mortlake & Preston
1989 to 1991
Sales Assistant

Education and training

- NVQ level 3 Customer Service
- Professional Development Award in Supervisory Management
- Six GCSEs including Maths and English

Personal details

Date of Birth: 19 April 1973
Health: Non-smoker
Interests: Active member of local athletics team, entered for 2002
             London Marathon
Licence: Full, clean UK driving licence
Prepared to relocate to any part of the country

The creative CV

Creative people are the problem-solvers within a company. If you're applying for a job in a creative sphere, make sure your CV highlights your:

- track record of effective, creative solutions;
- understanding of your specific field or discipline;
- background and experience;
- ability to work both independently and as part of a bigger team;
- flexibility and reliability.

Example CV – for a creative job

BEN ABATTA
7 North Side
Weston Stoke Hamden, Bucks BU11 5CP
Tel: 00000 000000
e-mail: abattab@anyisp.co.uk

Career profile

An innovative and intelligent exhibition designer with a sound understanding of detailed specification, planning and budgeting, liaising with internal and external clients and contractors, and a background in exhibition and display design for both private and local-authority clients.

Key experience

- Inclusive renovation of Museum galleries, having responsibility for:
  – Design and implementation
  – Planning and budgeting
  – Materials specification and purchasing
  – Managing construction team and local contractors
- Successful design and planning of more than a dozen feature exhibitions – one every six months
- Devising the innovative 'Museum-in-a-box', which allows exhibits to be toured to schools and displayed attractively, safely and informatively

- Designing, specifying and supervising interior renovation of museum annex to give café space and overspill gallery
- Bringing projects in on time and on budget and contributing to the award-winning success of the City Museum

Career history

1995 to Present
City Museum
Exhibition Designer
Designed custom-built gallery and feature displays for the Museum and for special touring exhibitions:

- Assessed requirements of exhibition and liaised with curators and experts to achieve the best results
- Designed attractive 'customer-friendly' displays
- Drew up fully detailed plans and instructions for installation by construction team
- Supervised final stages, layout and finish
- Maintained, renovated and updated displays

1990 to 1995
C J Handey
Chief Display Designer
Display Designer
Carried out in-store displays, promotions and window dressing as part of display team for major city-centre department store. As Chief Display Designer, personally responsible for designing annual Christmas Shop and main windows for key merchandise and displays.

Education and training

Westbourne University College
Foundation Diploma in Art and Design
BA (Hons) 3D Design

St James' School
Six GCSEs including English and Design Technology

Personal details

Date of Birth:	29 May 1968
Interests:	Member of the Stoke Hamden Archaeological Society and South Bucks Historical Society
References:	Available on request

The practical CV

Companies rely on people to do the practical jobs such as maintenance, warehousing and deliveries, that mean everyone else can get on with their own work. When the position you're applying for is a practical one, make sure your CV emphasizes your:

- practical skills and capabilities;
- hands-on experience;
- reliability;
- competence;
- ability to follow instructions and procedures;
- ability, also, to think for yourself and use your intelligence;
- vocational or job-related training, such as an NVQ.

Example CV – for a practical job

Rosa McCarthy
41 Plymouth Close
Saltflats, Salthaven, Dorset, DS3 6ZP
Tel: 00000 000000

Career profile

A trained, professional, highly competent waitress/hospitality assistant, with experience in both 5-star and fast-paced high-profile environments, now looking for a position that will provide the opportunity to undertake a (part-time) BTEC Diploma in Hospitality and Catering Services.

Key skills
- NVQ 2 Food Service
- A la carte and table d'hôte service
- Silver and French-style service
- Serve wine, spirits and other beverages
- Set tables for up to eight courses
- Take customer orders and liaise with kitchen
- Deal with customer enquiries, requests and complaints appropriately

Employment history
1999 to Present
Country Manor Hotel
Waitress
- Catered for a wide range of corporate and social functions
- Provided dining room service for 200 guests
- Served at banquets and special events
- Provided room service

1997 to 1999
Java
Waitress
Bar Staff
- Served customers in high-pressured high-fashion restaurant
- Served all types of beverages including cocktails
- Performed nightly total and reconciliation of bar till

Education and training
1995 to 1997 Thornbury CFE
NVQ levels 1&2 in Food Service

1989 to 1995 Thornbury Park School
Five GCSEs including English

Personal details
Date of Birth:	5 August 1977
Health:	Excellent. Non-smoker
Interests:	Badminton, aerobics, foreign travel

5

SPECIAL CONSIDERATIONS

Every individual's CV will be different, of course, depending on what they've done and what sort of job they want to do. But some CVs have special requirements and need individual consideration.

CVs for school and college leavers

When you're just leaving education and have very little experience, what do you put in your CV?

- **Career objective**. Use it to give a clear idea of where you are heading, along with your key strengths and positive qualities.
- **Qualifications**. Without experience, your qualifications are the most important thing you have to offer, so cover them in detail.
- **Achievements**. Highlight any achievements, duties or responsibilities you've undertaken.

- **Work experience**. Include *any* work experience you have – paid, part-time, voluntary work, work-experience placement, Saturday jobs, holiday jobs – it all helps to establish you are familiar with the working environment.

Example CV – school leaver

PAUL ROBBINS
98 St Brides Place
Portbury
South Devon, DV14 3XO
Tel: 00000 000000

Career objective
A friendly, outgoing school leaver with experience in retail. Dependable, trustworthy and able to work responsively with customers, with a good general education and a particular interest in retail work, sales or marketing.

Employment experience
LocoNet Convenience Stores
2000–Present
Sales Assistant
- Served and assisted customers
- Dealt with enquiries and complaints
- Handled cash
- Administered alcohol, tobacco and lottery legislation
- Worked evening shift and covered for sickness and staff absence on evenings and weekends

Harbour Galleries
Summer 2001
Sales Assistant
- Dealt with enquiries
- Took details of customer orders
- Arranged deliveries
- Maintained display areas

Education
1994–2001 Portbury Lees School
Intermediate GNVQ – Media Studies
GCSEs – English, German, History grade B, Maths grade C, Art,
General Science grade D

Computer skills
Familiar with everyday use, including word-processing, Internet use, etc.
Some use of spreadsheets and databases.

Personal details
Date of birth	7 April 1983
Health	Non-smoker
Interests	Member of local youth orchestra
Licence	Car owner/driver with full, clean UK licence

Example CV – college leaver

WILLIAM KENDAL
61 Aston Drive
Lodway
Surrey SR2 1PG
Tel: 00000 000000
e-mail: wkendal@anyisp.co.uk

Career objective
A well-motivated college leaver with employment experience and a
recently completed BTEC National Diploma in Computing, looking
for a position that provides the opportunity to continue to build further experience in this area.

Education and training
1999–2001 Surrey College
BTEC National Diploma in Computing
Specializing in:
Networking and ICT Support
The course covered all aspects of computing, including:

- Computer Systems
- Communications Technology
- Computational Methods
- Software Development
- Programming Practice
- Network Design and Administration

1992–1999 Priory Park School
A levels: Maths
GCSEs: Seven including Maths and IT

Work experience
1999–Present Potterdean Stores
Sales Assistant
- Served and assisted customers
- Handled cash
- Dealt with enquiries and complaints

1999–Present Surrey College
Administrative Assistant (voluntary part-time)
- Maintained files and records
- Undertook printing, photocopying and franking
- Carried out routine administrative work

Personal details
Date of birth: 1 May 1981
Licence: Full, clean UK driving licence
Interests: Reading, swimming, music, computers;
                 I have recently completed a Web site for Priory
                 House Athletics Team

For another example of a college/university leaver's CV, see
John Felling's on page 22.

CVs after a career break

What do you put in your CV when you return to work after a break, for whatever reason – childcare, travel, retraining, etc?

- **Career objective**. You can use this to connect the three parts of your working life – your previous employment, your experience during the break, and your future direction.

- **Key skills**. Include:
  - new skills gained through voluntary or part-time work;
  - qualifications and skills gained through education or training during your break;
  - anything else you've done to improve or update your skills and qualifications;
  - ways in which you've kept up to date with developments in your trade or profession;
  - positive ways in which you've changed: increased maturity, for example more responsible, confident, understanding, with new skills, insight, etc.

- **Career history**. Include any work you've done during your break, including part-time and voluntary work, or any special responsibilities or duties. Be positive about your return to employment and about what you've gained from your period outside it.

Example CV – returning after a career break

IONE CLARKE
61 Golden Hurst
Market Stoke, Kent KE20 5VO
Tel: 00000 000000
E-mail: iclarke@anyisp.co.uk

Career objective

A capable and professional **Human Resources Manager** with a primary
interest in training and development in the workplace, keen to use these
skills and expertise for the benefit of a company committed to getting the
best from their staff.

Key skills and experience

- Substantial experience of all facets of human resource evaluation
  and development
- Highly developed personnel management skills
- Experienced in formulating, delivering and assessing training
  programmes
- Trained and experienced in the use of psychometric and aptitude
  tests
- Comprehensive knowledge of employment law
- Widespread contacts within training and other agencies

Career history

1998 to Present
Women's Work Resource Centre
Voluntary Counsellor
- Set up and administered training and job-search advice service for
  single parents and women returning to the workplace
- Networked with local TEC and FEFC about training opportunities
  and funding
- Achieved average of 83 per cent success rate for those wishing to
  return to education or the workplace

1992 to 1998
Escol Orbit Ltd
Human Resources Manager
Complete personnel function for both office and manufacturing staff:

47

- Supervised introduction of performance evaluation system
- Developed personnel policies and procedures for office management group
- Enhanced implementation of human resource development programme
- Set up and managed Outplacement Service as part of redundancy programme resulting in 75 per cent success rate for those wishing to continue with employment

1987 to 1992
North West Group Ltd – Scottish Region
Personnel Officer
- Inclusive personnel function for regional centre staff
- Key role in introducing and implementing computerized personnel data system
- Administered records, pay and contractual documents

1981 to 1997
Prestlake Mortenson
Personnel Assistant
Clerical Officer
Clerical Assistant

Education and training

Fellow of the Institute of Personnel Management

Tollgate College
Diploma in Personnel Management

Work related training:
- Psychometric testing
- Aptitude testing
- Assessment skills
- Career guidance and counselling

Personal details

Date of birth	3 May 1963
Interests	Fine art and antiques, watercolour painting
Health	Non-smoker
Licence	Car owner/driver with full UK driving licence

For other examples of people returning to work after a break, see Sylvia Patterson's on page 20, and Joy Perris's (Example 2 – after) on page 11.

CVs for career changers

What do you put in your CV when you're changing direction, whether it's because of retraining, altered circumstances, new priorities, or changes in the job market?

- **Career objective**. Use a career objective at the top of your CV to make your new career direction absolutely clear. Use it to connect the three parts of your working life – your previous employment, the reason for the change, and your future direction.
- **Key skills/experience/qualities/achievements**.
  Pick out the key points that best illustrate your suitability for your new direction:
  – existing skills and experience that would be useful in your new career;
  – new qualifications and skills gained through education or training;
  – the personal qualities that make you right for this new job.
- **Career history**. Be positive but brief about your career history. Use it to give a picture of you rather than itemizing duties and responsibilities not relevant to your future direction.

Example CV – changing careers

MARK ORWELL
Flat 4, Picton House
Cornwell Street, Baybury
Somerset SM15 3BI
Tel: 00000 000000

Career objective
To employ and develop my existing skills, qualifications and experience
of working with people in a challenging, stimulating and worthwhile
counselling-related situation, where there is also a prospect of ongoing
personal development and learning.

Key qualifications
Certificate of Counselling Practice (AEB)
Certificate of Counselling Theory (AEB)

Career history
1998 to Present
Marshfield Project
Volunteer Counsellor
- Counselled young people with a variety of problems centring on
  homelessness
- Worked alongside Social Services implementing general policy as
  well as working on specific cases
- Managed a heavy caseload including crisis intervention
- Gave advice and information on housing and benefit entitlements
- Participated in supervision and support meetings
- Attended residential course on Means Tested Benefit by the Welfare
  Rights Unit

1996 to 1998
Mereside Health Trust
Patient Services Transport Driver
Provided driver support for local ring and ride scheme covering two dis-
trict outpatient departments, three clinics and three day centres.
Collected patients from home and took to destination, assisting special
needs patients on and off vehicle.

1994 to 1996
Southwest Consumables
Delivery Driver
Delivered products to local businesses, maintained delivery records, schedules and logs.

1990 to 1994
Various
Provided temporary and short-contract cover in construction and delivery work

Education and training
Southwest CFE
● Certificate of Counselling Practice (AEB)
● Certificate of Counselling Theory (AEB)

Handcross School
● Six GCSEs including Maths and English
● GNVQ Construction and the Built Environment

Personal details
Date of birth   1 March 1974
Interests   Marathon running; hill walking and climbing
References   Available on request

The online CV

If you find a vacancy on the Internet, you'll usually be asked to apply online.

CVs sent via the Internet or stored in online databases follow the same rules as any other CV, namely:

● Keep it short.

● Keep it simple (so the important details stand out).

● Keep it 'reader friendly'.

● Keep it relevant.

A few points, however, apply to online CVs that don't necessarily affect CVs sent through the mail:

- Many organizations are wary of opening files from an unknown source, so sending your CV as an attached file could be a problem. Instead, keep it in the main body of your text.

- If you *are* sending your CV as an attached file, include your own name in the file name, ie johnsmithcv.doc. Organizations receive dozens of files just called cv.doc.

- Fill in the subject line. It's usual to put the job title and/or reference number that appear in the ad.

- Don't take up valuable screen space with your name and e-mail address, these will appear at the top of the page anyway. Start with the main part of your CV – your Personal statement followed by your Key skills/ Experience – and put your home address and telephone number in with your Personal details.

- Stick to standard fonts for your e-mailed CV, otherwise it could be unreadable.

- You will need to edit your CV so that it still looks good on the small screen. An e-mail screen displays much less than a sheet of A4 paper – only about 20 lines at a time. The first screen that comes up will also have your name, e-mail address and subject details at the top, which leaves even less space – about 10 lines – for the key information about your skills and experience. Bear this in mind when planning your CV:

  - Make it concise. A two-page CV can run to six or seven screens online.

  - Arrange information in screen-sized chunks, rather than splitting it, so it appears in easy-to-read sections.

- If you're certain your recipient can receive HTML format, you can paste in your CV complete with bullet points, bold, italics, etc. However, some computers only present e-mail as plain text, so don't rely on formatting. Instead, use capital letters and spacing to present the information clearly.

- Look at your CV in the outbox to get an employer's eye view before sending it off.

It's reasonably easy to adapt your CV so that it still looks good even in plain text. The following example shows Roger Harup's CV on page 32 adapted from formatted to plain text for e-mail.

Example CV – changed to plain text for e-mail

Subject:	Regional Executive Application
Date:	Thu, 6 July 2001 14:33:10 – 0900
From:	Roger Harup <harupr@anyisp.com>
To:	Progers@meadiapress.co.uk

A sales professional with extensive experience in sales, marketing and management, the skill and confidence to identify and generate sales leads from a diverse project base, and a positive attitude towards the future

>>KEY EXPERIENCE
~ Diploma in marketing and e-commerce
~ Three years running an international sales office
~ Familiarity with export and UK commercial regulation
~ Increased territory sales by 25 per cent in current position
~ Increased net sales by 43 per cent
----
this is roughly the end of the first screen

>>CAREER ACHIEVEMENTS

Staple & Dennis Ltd   1995–Present
COMMERCIAL MANAGER
Responsible for Northern European sales operations
~ Recruited, motivated and developed staff
~ Developed training and incentives
~ Selected and trained representatives for overseas territories
~ Managed existing accounts while developing new ones
~ Maintained long-term customer relationships
~ Increased repeat orders by 37 per cent
~ Planned and controlled sales resources to maximum effect

Dakk Taylor & Co Ltd   1992–1995
SALES/PRODUCT MANAGER
~ Increased sales year-on-year by up to 33 per cent
~ Maintained cash flow and profitability
~ Analysed and evaluated sales results
~ Maintained profitability of product range alongside new ones

----
this is roughly the end of the second screen

PortMarine Ltd   1988–1992
SALES MANAGER
SALES REPRESENTATIVE
~ Increased sales turnover
~ Introduced new products and marketing ideas
~ Recruited and trained sales team
~ Promoted to Sales Manager in 1990

>>EDUCATION

Institute of Continuing Studies   1988–1992
~ Diploma in Marketing and E-Commerce
~ Diploma in Computing and IT

Stoke Croft School   1981–1988
~ A-level Maths and Economics
~ Six GCSEs including Maths and English

>>PERSONAL DETAILS

Date of birth: 16 February 1970
Interests: IT and computing
Licence: Full, clean UK driving licence
Address: 68 Orion Close, Aspen Hill, Staffordshire ST4 8SM
Tel: 00000 000000

Scanning

Large organizations are, increasingly, using software to carry out a preliminary scan of CVs based on key word searches. If you know that your CV is going to be scanned, make it easy for an optical scanner to read it:

- Use plain white paper and print on one side only.
- Use a clear, standard 11- or 12-point font.
- Put your name at the top of each page, not just the first one.
- Don't staple or clip pages together.
- Send it unfolded in an A4 envelope – the scanner may try to read any fold lines.
- Bullet points, italics, bold, underlining, etc can baffle older scanning packages. Revise your CV accordingly.

The key words the scanner will be looking for are:

- **occupations** – teaching, engineering, public relations, retailing, financial management, quality control, customer care, etc;
- **positions** – manager, programmer, editor, engineer, director, etc;
- **specific skills and qualifications** – Microsoft Word, Windows NT, ISO90000, BSc, MA, etc;
- **workplace skills** – designed, evaluated, represented, organized, formulated, developed, etc.

Study the job advertisement or job description carefully and pull out the key words as a starting point.

Be specific. The job description may just ask for word-processing skills. Use the phrase 'word-processing' but add the specific skills you have as well – Word, PowerPoint etc.

Go into detail. If you are 'an IT professional with a range of skills gained providing support and development for Badbury Council Housing Management Team', give clear details of what, exactly, that post entails:

- Four years' experience as IT Development Officer
- Experience in Unix Operating System Administration
- Worked as an ORACLE DBA
- Wrote reports using Report Writer 2x
- Worked as part of project team

6

CV PROBLEMS

Problem: CV more than two pages long
Solution: highlight your *relevant* skills, give details of your *current* job and *recent* experience, and ruthlessly summarize everything else.

Problem: Gaps in career history
Solution: Smooth over small gaps by rounding up dates. For longer gaps, find something positive to say about what you were doing – training, study, taking a sabbatical, travelling, voluntary work, child-rearing, domestic commitments, self-employment, freelancing, consultancy work, etc.

Problem: Lots of different jobs; no clear career direction
Solution: Most skills are transferable – you will use interpersonal skills or organizational skills, for example, in a range of jobs. Pick out the *relevant* transferable skills you've acquired over a variety of jobs and list them in your Key skills or Key experience section, then choose the most relevant *specific* skills, qualifications or experience to

include as well. Briefly summarize your actual career history, emphasizing your use of these skills.

Problem: Current job isn't the most impressive/most relevant
Solution: As well as a Key skills section, consider introducing a Key experience section as well, and summarizing your career very briefly so that your skills and experience stand out far more strongly than your current position:

Key skills
List your skills relevant to the job you're applying for. For example:

● Developing new accounts while maintaining and cultivating existing ones
● Producing quarterly analyses of sales by product and customer

Key experience
List the experience and achievements you've gained in other, more relevant jobs. For example:

● Creating venture capital company and establishing profile in the United Kingdom
● Generating over £7 million of business with 18 months of launch
● Installing and implementing all administrative systems; administering all documentation, agreements and financial analyses

Career summary

Don't give details, just put:

2000–Present	Sales Manager	Zotech Ltd
1995–2000	Sales and Marketing Director	Aristo Ltd
1990–1995	Sales and Marketing Manager	P W Carr
1985–1990	Sales Executive	CallStream

Use your covering letter and the interview to explain, in as positive a light as possible, the reason for the setback – company merger, redundancy, or whatever.

Problem: Over-qualified

Solution: Stress your hands-on skills and experience relevant to the job you're applying for on the front page, and tuck your 'excess' qualifications away in the Education and training section on the second page.

Problem: Under-qualified

Solution: Very much like the one above. If you know you have the hands-on skills and experience to do the job even though they're asking for a graduate, for example, put the relevant key points on the front page.

Problem: Over 50

Solution: Emphasize your successful track record of achievements, include details of your last two or three positions and ruthlessly summarize your early career record:

Key skills and experience

- Ten years' experience in electrical engineering
- Knowledge of installing, servicing and repairing electro-mechanical and electronic equipment
- Understanding of precision instrumentation
- Established track record of staff supervision

Career history
1995 to Present
Clarkson Electronics
Section Supervisor
Electrical Fitter
Include details of your current responsibilities and achieve-ments. For example:

● Repaired electronic and electro-mechanical equipment
● Performed and verified precision instrument calibration

1990 to 1995
Overlander Ltd
Electrical Maintenance Engineer
Include details about this job also. For example:

● Overhauled and maintained equipment
● Serviced overhead equipment
● Repaired high-speed machine tools

Prior to 1990
Various
Electrical Engineer
Package your early career history under one heading, giving an outline of the sort of work you did. Jobs you did more than a decade ago are not relevant to your current career.

Problem: Under 25
Solution: If you've been in further or higher education, you may be lacking in experience. Make the most of what you've got, highlighting skills gained at college or univer-sity whether or not you've had the chance to use them in the workplace.

7

USING YOUR CV

If you've taken time and care getting a really good CV together, don't leave it sitting on your desk, get it working for you by using the job-search methods below. The more strategies you use, the greater your chances of success.

Reply to advertisements

You can find advertised vacancies in:

● newspaper 'situations vacant' pages;
● Internet sites – either on company sites or specific job-search sites;
● the job pages in trade and professional journals;
● Job Centre vacancy boards.

Reading the appointments pages will give you a good overview of what's available, what's being asked for, the salaries available, etc. While these can be a useful source of information, remember that not all vacancies are actually advertised and that relying solely on this method of finding a job could limit your opportunities.

Job ads need to be read carefully before responding. You usually only have one chance to make an impression and your application needs to stand out strongly given that you will be in direct competition with everyone else who has applied. Answering advertised vacancies will work well for you if:

- you have an occupational magazine, journal or Web site that carries lots of good-quality job-ads;
- you have widely used skills;
- plenty of vacancies come up regularly in your field;
- you are looking for work in a specific location and can use the local paper or Job Centre.

Target employers

Send your CV plus a covering letter to employers you think will be interested in seeing you. Rather than sitting and waiting for a reply, follow it up with a phone call to see if you can set up an interview.

Do your preliminary research to find out which organizations to pursue and who to contact within the company. A CV and a call to a named individual who has the authority to interview you stand more chance of getting a response than one just sent to the personnel department. This method will appeal to you if:

- you have an excellent CV that sells your skills and accomplishments;
- you have a good idea of the market and the companies likely to be interested in your skills;
- you are confident about your value to an employer.

Enrol with a headhunter or agency

These can be very helpful, particularly if there is a specialist agency for your type of work, and they have the advantage of knowing the job market well and:

● they know what's happening and can make informed guesses about what might happen in the future;

● they know where the jobs are;

● they know who to contact;

● they have an established track record with employers.

Prepare your CV for an agency as carefully as you would for an employer. You are still, in effect, aiming to be selected for interview as they will be assessing your suitability for various positions on the strength of what they see. In order to keep your file 'fresh', keep in regular contact and update them frequently. An agency will be especially useful to you if:

● you have widely marketable skills;

● you have a track record of experience in your field;

● you are prepared to keep in regular contact.

Network

This method uses your professional and social contacts to help you get in touch with potential employers who might not otherwise be so accessible. The people and organizations in your network can help you by:

● giving you information about potential vacancies, changes within organizations, etc;

● passing your CV to people with the authority to interview;

● allowing their name to be used as an introduction;

● introducing you personally;

- speaking to others on your behalf;
- recommending you either in person or in writing.

This strategy will work well for you if:

- you have a wide network of contacts, or the potential exists to develop one;
- you have access to 'ready made' networks such as trade and professional associations;
- you are good at following up leads and introductions;
- you are happy to build relationships and pay back favours when the time comes.